THE DOWN-GOING OF ORPHEUS HAWKINS

A children's play

DAVID CLARKE

With Music by

MAVIS DUNSTON

SAMUEL FRENCH

FRENCH

LONDON

NEW YORK   TORONTO   SYDNEY   HOLLYWOOD

INTRODUCTION

To read the Greek myths is to enter a world of magic and wonder, and one of the most enchanting and imaginative of these stories is the legend of Orpheus and Eurydice, upon which *The Down-Going of Orpheus Hawkins* is very loosely based.

The play was first staged in April 1968, and has since been performed by schools in Leeds, Cambridge, Manchester, and Sandbach. Its first performance was given by a cast made up entirely of 11-year-old boys and girls, but it was written with the 11–14 age group in mind, because the range of choice of suitable material for pupils of this age is somewhat restricted.

The first act of the play is rather episodic in construction. To achieve a smooth flow there should therefore be no break between the end of one scene and the start of another. Changes of scene are indicated by changes in lighting, or music, or mood, or by the prompt appearance of different characters, or by a combination of these factors.

The Down-Going of Orpheus Hawkins provides opportunity in production for a full range of theatre arts including dance, mime, and music. This working script is intended to be flexible and allow producers to amend and adapt the material as necessary. The play's large cast gives scope for everyone, and it can be read with enjoyment in the classroom.

D.C.

NOTES

Aristaeus (see page 12), in classical mythology, was the god of beekeeping. He had dishonourable intentions towards Eurydice. It was while she was fleeing from his unwelcome designs upon her that she trod on a snake, which bit her ankle and so caused her to die.

A guide to the pronunciation of the Greek names will be found at the end of the text on page 41.

The fairground scene (page 13). Ten years ago, for a production of the melodrama *Maria Marten*, or *The Murder in the Red Barn*, I was asked to write a short alternative scene to Act 1 Scene 3 of the Barnstormers' Edition of that play. (The play is published by Heinemann Educational Books Ltd, and is edited by Montagu Slater.) This fairground scene is an adaptation of the scene that I originally wrote for *Maria Marten*, and includes one or two lines from the text of the melodrama.

D.C.

MUSIC

The music to the play was written for performance by four eleven-year-old children, a guitarist and a pianist. The string players were inexperienced, hence the simplicity of their parts. The recorder and percussion players were most competent and consequently have the most demanding melodies.

It is possible to double up on the parts, but more than eight performers (excluding piano) may cause problems of "balance" especially in the solo songs.

The accompaniment to *My Home is the Forest* in Act I is for guitar or piano.

In Act II the Mourners sing *Down, Down into the Depths* several times. It would be more effective to leave them unaccompanied in certain of these. Their voices may be supplemented, as may all the other songs in the play, by a "Greek chorus" or choir situated off stage (in the orchestra pit).

There is scope, especially in Act II, for adapting this music for background sounds, or for mime and dance, or even for composing your own.

M.M.D.

Separate parts are written for recorder
                                   violin
                                  'cello
                                percussion
Piano and guitar play from the full score.

Copies of the music are obtainable from Samuel French Ltd.

CAST

The First Storyteller
The Second Storyteller
The Producer
Mrs Calliope Hawkins
Orpheus Hawkins
Eurydice Dalyrymple
Pyramus McPrawn
Thisbe Longbottom
Harry, a technician
The Third Storyteller
Charon, the ferryman of the dead
Minos ⎤
Rhadamanthus ⎬ Judges of the Underworld
Aeacus ⎦
Hades, King of the Underworld
A Detective
First Showman
Second Showman
Third Showman
Fourth Showman
Fifth Showman
Sixth Showman
First Wood Nymph
Second Wood Nymph
Third Wood Nymph
First Villager
Second Villager
Third Villager
Fourth Villager
First Spirit
Second Spirit
Persephone, Queen of the Underworld
Wood Nymphs and Woodland Animals
Three Ordinary Mourners
Nine Mourners from the Underworld
Villagers, Fairground Crowd, Underworld Spirits,
Dancers, Voices, Singers, etc.

The action of the play passes in a present-day theatre

MUSICAL NUMBERS

ACT I

1	*I Love the Stars*	Orpheus, Wood Nymphs, Woodland Animals
2	*Green and Gold*	Wood Nymphs, Woodland Animals
3	*My Home is the Forest*	Eurydice, Wood Nymphs, Woodland Animals
4	*All the Fun of the Fair*	Crowd

ACT II

5	*Bluebells*	Orpheus
6	*Down, Down into the Depths*	Mourners, Eurydice
7	*Down, Down into the Depths* (reprise)	Mourners, Eurydice
8	*O Spirit of Death*	Orpheus
9	*O Spirit of Death* (part reprise)	Orpheus

ACT I

Scene 1

The stage is bare except for two or three levels which sweep down towards the audience. Steps lead down from the highest level on the left of the stage to the front of the apron. There are steps down from the apron to the aisles R, L *and* C

The First Storyteller enters R. *He is full of self-importance. This is his great moment*

First Storyteller (*hamming*) This is an old tale. And not a happy one. But full of woe, alas, and pain, the darkness of a winter day. This tale—it has the quality of ancient stones. It is as old as the dawn. It is set for ever among the weeping constellations.

The Second Storyteller hurries down the aisle C

Second Storyteller Sorry I'm late. Couldn't get a bus. I've been waiting ages. Then I got off at the wrong stop. By jove, it's getting chilly out. (*He smacks and rubs his hands. A pause while the Storytellers look at each other*) Sorry, don't let me interrupt. (*He takes off his coat and hangs it on a peg on the proscenium arch* L. *It remains there throughout the play in full view of the audience*)

First Storyteller I'd just got to the bit about the constellations.

Second Storyteller Oh, yes. We've started then. (*He sits down on the steps* L C)

First Storyteller Yes. Right. (*Remembering*) For ever among the weeping constellations. This legendary tale stirs the sorrow in every human heart, for like a hill . . .

Second Storyteller Hadn't you better tell them about constellations?

First Storyteller Pardon?

Second Storyteller You'd better tell them about constellations. There may be some people here with very young children. They won't know what constellations means.

First Storyteller Who?

Second Storyteller The children!

First Storyteller It doesn't matter. It's not very important.

Second Storyteller Of course it matters. (*He takes an apple from his pocket, rubs it on the sleeve of his jacket, and takes a big bite*) How would you like to be brought here by the scruff of the neck and not understand a word of what's going on?

First Storyteller I thought it would be obvious what constellations means. Anyway, it isn't a play suitable for very young children. It is a modern interpretation of a Greek myth.

Second Storyteller Yes, oh yes, that's all right! Hey! Get 'em here, take their money, and then tell them it's not suitable. That's commercialism for you!

First Storyteller (*getting angry*) Now look here. I've a job to do. You aren't helping. You're not an actor. You were supposed to look after the machines, and not going poking your nose into other people's affairs.

Second Storyteller I just object to people being cheated, that's all.

First Storyteller So who's being cheated?

Second Storyteller Bringing them all this way. They could have stayed in and watched telly.

First Storyteller All I said was, that the play isn't suitable for very young children. I can say that, can't I? It's a free country. I can say that, can't I?

Second Storyteller If it's in the script.

First Storyteller It isn't in the script. I'm still waiting to start the script if you'll just get on with the machines!

Second Storyteller Right, I will.

First Storyteller Right. (*To the audience*) The fact is that this play is not very suitable for young children. (*He is obviously ruffled*) Now, where were we?

Second Storyteller Constellations. Stars, that is.

First Storyteller Oh yes. Now. This legendary tale—this legendary tale stirs the sorrow in every human heart. It has the shape of willows, mournful and sad. Or like a hill, stark and despairing, it turns its proud head to an unsmiling sky The voice of this tale crosses the centuries, and tells . . .

Second Storyteller You're only eleven, anyway.

First Storyteller Pardon?

Second Storyteller I said, "you're only eleven, anyway".

First Storyteller (*completely bewildered*) What are you—I know I'm only eleven. What's that got to do with it? What are you talking about?

Second Storyteller Well, some people would say that you are a bit on the young side. If this play is so unsuitable, *you* ought not to be here.

First Storyteller Oh, now look here.

Second Storyteller No, it's true. If you are very young, you need a licence. You need a special licence from the police, if you want to get on a stage. If you are very young that is.

First Storyteller (*with mounting anger*) Look, I'm the narrator. I'm telling the story. I'm getting a bit sick of your interfering. This didn't happen at rehearsals. You were supposed to look after the machines. (*He counts off the points as he makes them on his fingers*) So I haven't got a licence. The play will be over before ten o'clock. So I don't need a licence even if I did need one! The play is not suitable for very young children. I mean toddlers, tiny tots that high—(*he makes a gesture*)—not

yet out of their prams. So I'm only eleven. (*With supreme irony*) Grand-
father, how old are you?

Second Storyteller (*very deliberately*) Twelve.

First Storyteller (*totally baffled*) Twelve! Then what . . .

Second Storyteller But I'm very mature for my age. I don't laugh at the
rude bits.

First Storyteller There aren't any rude bits! It's a Greek play about
Pyramus and Thisbe and there aren't any rude bits.

Second Storyteller What! Then why isn't it suitable for very young
children? What's all this pretence? What are you trying to hide?

First Storyteller It wasn't, isn't suitable for very young children because
it is a tragedy. (*He is at his wits' end with anger, and shouts at the top
of his voice*) It is a tragedy. Do you hear me? And you have spoilt it.
You have ruined it completely. Are you glad, eh? Are you glad you've
spoilt it? You were supposed to look after the machines. Did you know
that? Did you? Well, I've had enough. I've had enough. I've had a
basinful! (*He pulls a script from his pocket and hurls it to the ground*)
Enough is enough. I am off.

Second Storyteller Look, I didn't mean to upset you.

First Storyteller (*moving back up the steps of the apron*) Upset! Upset! I'm
not upset! Whatever gave you that idea? (*He walks quickly down aisle C*)
All I can say is that whoever brought you into the play must have been
mental. Right off his rocker. (*To the audience*) And you, I wonder how
you people can stand it.

Second Storyteller Hey, come back.

First Storyteller Not on your life. I didn't come here to be insulted. "I'll
be revenged on the whole pack of you!"

The First Storyteller exits

Second Storyteller Very temperamental. Very temperamental. (*He picks
up the discarded script*) Well, I suppose I'd better go and look after
these machines.

The Second Storyteller exits

SCENE 2

*Lights flicker and go on and off. A rocket is fired and explodes. It is followed
by a line or two of* Nymphs and Shepherds, Come Away. *An express train
at full belt thunders through the loudspeakers. A dinner gong reverberates
through the auditorium as the House Lights come up*

The Producer comes on, examining a script

Producer I'm sorry about this, ladies and gentlemen. Something has happened which doesn't appear to be in the script. Pyramus and Thisbe should be on now. If you'll wait just a moment. Talk if you want to.

The Producer exits

Brass band music is heard, rising to a crescendo

The Producer enters

The brass band music fades away

Ladies and gentlemen . . .

Mrs Hawkins, about half-way back in the stalls, stands up

Mrs Hawkins Here, you.

Producer I'm sorry. A temporary fault. I can't find them anywhere.

Mrs Hawkins Here you. What's all this messing about? I came here to see a play. It's supposed to be about Pie-rarm-us and This Bee, I think.

Producer (*correcting*) Pyramus and Thisbe.

Mrs Hawkins That's right. Well get on with it.

Producer Well you see, our Narrator has walked out, so we can't very well get on with it. If you will just be patient . . .

Mrs Hawkins Patient! I didn't come here to be patient. I came to see a play.

Producer Perhaps some Community Singing . . .

Mrs Hawkins This is daylight robbery! Never you mind your fol-de-rol-days! Just get on with the play.

Producer (*turning nasty*) Oh, I suppose you can do better! Your sort always can.

Mrs Hawkins Ah, we're getting personal now, are we?

Producer The likes of you, Madam, are better locked up.

Mrs Hawkins I'm not standing for that.

Producer Well go on. Clear off. We don't want your sort in here, thank you very much.

Mrs Hawkins Very polite, I'm sure. Very courteous. I've paid for this seat.

Producer Well sit in it and shut up! I'm having difficulties enough trying to sort out the cast without you butting your nose into other people's affairs.

Mrs Hawkins You're a lout. That's what you are. You're a lout.

Producer Get out of this theatre, you—you washerwoman! Go on! Out!

Mrs Hawkins Orpheus!

Orpheus Yes, Mum?

Mrs Hawkins Come on, son. We're going.

Orpheus, who has been sitting next to his mother in the middle of the row, stands up

Orpheus Yes, Mum. Why, Mum.

Producer (*visibly surprised*) Orpheus—did you say? Orpheus?
Mrs Hawkins Come on, Orpheus. We're going home. Excuse me, please.
I've never been spoken to like that, never. (*They move down the row*)
Thank you. Thank you. A downright disgrace. (*To the Producer*) I shall
report you!

*Mrs Hawkins turns away with Orpheus. Orpheus is reluctant to go and stands
arguing*

Producer Orpheus! It might be possible! A spontaneous creation! It
might just be possible! An improvisation! Delete Pyramus and Thisbe.
Insert Orpheus. An improvisation based on all the latest theories of
educational drama! Characters playing themselves! (*He prances with
excitement*) It's what I've always wanted to do! Fame, fame! A Knight-
hood! Oh joy, joy! (*He calls out to Mrs Hawkins and her son*) Stay,
er—friends! Friends, friends! Perhaps I have been rather hasty. The
truth is, in my anxiety I say rash things. I do apologize. It was very
foolish of me. (*Pause*) I wonder, Madam, if your splendid boy—
Orpheus, did you say?—would like to see back stage? Perhaps we
could even find a small part for him!
Mrs Hawkins Well, er—I don't know—I don't think so . . .
Orpheus Oh yes. May I, Mum? Please, Mum. Please. Oh, go on, Mum.
Mrs Hawkins (*making her mind up firmly*) No! (*She grabs Orpheus's arm*)
Producer (*equally firmly*) Yes! (*He grabs Orpheus's other arm*).
Orpheus (*in pain at being stretched out*) Argh! Oh, please, Mum!
Producer (*very melodramatically*) Can't you see the Boy wants to?

Mrs Hawkins releases her grip

Have you no Heart, O Cruel Woman? Must you direct your Monstrous
Anger upon the Fragile Head of one So Young? Can you not weep?
Have you no Sorrow, no Spirit of Compassion? O, Woman of Stone,
relent! Find Pity in your Bosom, the Courage to say, "Yes!"
Mrs Hawkins Well, if you put it like that . . .
Producer I do! I do! I do! Up these steps my son. Ha! A fine lad, a fine
lad! Off you go, that way, yes. Ask the Technician to show you around.
I'll be with you in a moment. (*He turns to Mrs Hawkins*) Now,
Madam, most gracious lady, if you would care to return to your seat.
No, the Royal Box, I think. (*He calls into the wings*) Harry, a chair! I can
assure you that Orpheus will derive much benefit from this experience.
A fine lad, yes. And thank you so much.

*The Producer is all smiles and gratitude. He shows Mrs Hawkins into the
wings*

Ladies and Gentlemen! We appear to have solved a major problem.
Just a little re-shuffling of the cast is all that is necessary and I think I
can say you will be pleased with our amended production. By a stroke
of good luck, call it fate if you like, our Theatre Manager, who is at
present touring with Billy Smart's Circus, has a daughter, Eurydice—
one of our usherettes. I'm sure you'll agree that Orpheus and she will

make a lovely couple. Neither of them has appeared on stage before, so
you might say that this is their Golden Opportunity. If you'll excuse
me, we'll be ready in a moment. Yes!

The Producer goes off

SCENE 3

*The sound of heavy marching feet is heard through the loudspeakers. A
gong booms out. The loudspeaker announces: "Attention please, Attention,
please. Here are the team changes." It is followed by a terrific crash, groans
and then silence*

*The Stage Lights and House Lights, which have flickered oddly, now finally
go out*

*Music is heard, a gay pastoral. The Wood Nymphs (including Eurydice)
enter, and the Woodland Animals. The Lights come up slowly on a woodland
scene. There is a dance, then piping cries of "Orpheus" from the Woodland
Animals, as Orpheus comes on. They crowd round him and sing*

Song: "I LOVE THE STARS"

Orpheus   *(singing)*
Wood Nymphs   I love the stars, I love the moon,
Woodland   I love the earth, each tree and stone,
Animals   Each flower, bird, the sun, the sea,
                       The wind that whispers over me.

                       This is a magic in this land,
                       The sort of magic you will find
                       In fairy tales and legends old,
                       The deeds of giants, and heroes bold.

Solo   And so I sing, for my great love
                       Is just in wandering beneath these groves:
                       To play, to sing, to smile, to sleep,
                       To dream of Fortune in dark woods deep.

Chorus   We love the stars, we love the moon,
                       We love the earth, each tree and stone,
                       Each flower, bird, the sun, the sea,
                       Each wind that whispers, "Life is Free".

                       And so we sing, for our great love
                       Is just in wandering beneath these groves:
                       To play, to sing, to smile, to sleep,
                       To dream of Fortune in dark woods deep.

They gather flowers and bring them to Eurydice. There is a happy, comic dance from four Woodland Animals, but the music suddenly acquires a menacing tone. All freeze as a voice like the wind whispers through the wood

Voice Orpheus, Orpheus. Beware. Beware the Fate of the Dreamer. Beware the King of the Shadows. Orpheus, Orpheus . . .

The voice dies away, and is answered by a hollow, mocking laugh

The Wood Nymphs and Woodland Animals flee with tiny cries

Eurydice tries to run away

Orpheus Come back! (*He catches hold of Eurydice as she tries to run away, and calls after them*) It was to me the voice spoke. Don't be afraid. I will protect you.

Eurydice cowers away

I have heard that voice many times since I came back home with Jason and the Argonauts. (*Pause*) Come, I will not harm you. Who are you? What is your name? Are you a Wood Nymph?

Eurydice Eurydice.

Orpheus Eurydice. Your name sounds like a spell.

Eurydice You are Orpheus.

Orpheus Yes. I roam these lands, making music in praise of the gods. But I first won fame as a warrior in search of the Golden Fleece.

Eurydice I have heard tales of that great voyage. (*Pause*) I must go.

Orpheus No.

Eurydice I must.

Orpheus No. Stay.

During his last words a light chase begins. Eurydice moves quickly and nimbly but gracefully. Each time she tries to escape Orpheus bars the way. Her attempts to escape become a game

Eurydice I cannot. I must go.

Orpheus Got you!

Eurydice I must go.

Some of the Wood Nymphs and Woodland Animals return

Orpheus You are very beautiful, Eurydice.

Eurydice You are—mortal!

Orpheus Come, I'll take you hunting, and you shall see the village where I live.

Eurydice I am afraid of your world. I belong here among the trees and ferns. I am part of the woodland.

Orpheus There is nothing to be afraid of. They believe me. They understand.

Eurydice The fields are my home. I must stay here.

Orpheus Can't you persuade her? Listen.

Song: "GREEN AND GOLD"

Wood Nymphs ⎫ (*singing*)
Woodland Animals ⎭ In green and gold is the year returning,
The crocus blows when the winds awake;
Speak not of fear, for the gods are burning
Green and gold for true love's sake.

The daffodils all in gold are burning,
The warrior leaves hold up bright shields;
Young is the year, for the gods returning
Have cast in green the winter fields.

Then be not sad for this green appearing,
The gods true love never will forsake;
No cause for tears, when the young endearing
Time turns love gold, and woods awake.

In green and gold is the year returning,
The crocus blows when the winds awake;
We'll have no fear, for the gods are burning
Green and gold for true love's sake.

Orpheus Come on. Let's go hunting.
Eurydice I cannot—but come again, soon. Tell me your adventures.

   Eurydice runs out

Orpheus I will. Tomorrow, (*he calls after her*) I'll be here. Wait for me.

He sees the Woodland Animals and frightens them away again by making a sudden great shout

   They flee with squeaks, and Orpheus goes out happily

SCENE 4

The Stage Lights brighten

Two grotesque human beings enter: Pyramus, who is small, fat, and red, and Thisbe, who is extremely tall and pale-faced, with long ginger hair straggling to her shoulders in knotted rats' tails. She carries a flower, which she twirls abstractedly. They take a long time to position themselves in exactly the right spot downstage, and then stand side by side facing the audience and doing absolutely nothing. Their faces are expressionless. After a while

Pyramus gives a tiny, childish wave to the audience, but there is no other movement

The First Storyteller enters, and launches into his major speech

First Storyteller This is an old tale . . . .

   He is quickly interrupted by the Second Storyteller who staggers on carrying an immense box

Second Storyteller It's the fairground scene soon. (*Shouting*) Is it the fairground scene soon? (*He attempts to peer round the box and into the wings*) Yes, I know I'm on the stage, but if you will put the things on the wrong side. You don't think I could get behind the cyc, with this, do you? (*He sees Pyramus and Thisbe for the first time. During the conversation which follows he does not attempt to put the box down, and all conversation takes place over, under, and round the sides of it*)

Pyramus is loud but harmless. Thisbe is rather like an ugly sister in pantomime, though she believes she is a beautiful heroine. She has more intelligence than Pyramus.

   Hello, what's this? Would you mind moving please? We're doing a play.
Pyramus Oh.

Pause

Thisbe Oh.
First Storyteller (*to Pyramus and Thisbe*) I told you it was a new play. I told you you weren't in it.
Second Storyteller Yes. There are plenty of seats down there.

Nobody moves. The Second Storyteller starts to go off, and then stops.

   I said there are plenty of seats down there. (*He comes back*) So would you mind . . .
Pyramus ⎱ (*in one sudden loud chorus*) Shan't! ⎰ (*Speaking together*)
Thisbe ⎰   ⎱
Second Storyteller But—but you'll have to. You can't watch the play from here. The seats are down there.
Pyramus I am Pyramus!
Thisbe I am Thisbe!
Second Storyteller Well, I'm very glad to meet you, but you can't stay here.
Pyramus We are in the play.
Second Storyteller Which play?
Thisbe The play we are in.
Second Storyteller Oh, well, that's all right. (*He starts to go off*)
First Storyteller This is an old tale. And not a happy one. But full of woe, alas, and pain . . .

The Second Storyteller stops, turns and comes back

Second Storyteller Er, just a minute.
First Storyteller What?
Second Storyteller We've already done that bit. We're getting ready for the fairground scene now.
First Storyteller Tell him.
Pyramus There is no fairground scene in our play.
Thisbe There is no fairground scene in our play.
Second Storyteller But I've got it here—in the box. The Fair, Roller-Coaster, Stalls, Sound Effects, Paper Hats, the lot!
First Storyteller Well our play is about Pyramus and Thisbe, so you won't need to use them, because . . . (*He turns and extends his arm with a flourish to Pyramus and Thisbe*)

The Producer enters

Pyramus
Thisbe } There is no fairground scene in our play! { (*Speaking together*)
Producer What's going on now? What are you doing here?
Pyramus Acting!
Thisbe In the play of Pyramus and Thisbe.
First Storyteller This is an old tale. And not a happy one. But full of woe . . .
Producer Just a minute. Let's get this sorted out. (*To the Second Storyteller*) Get those fairground effects set up, will you?

The Second Storyteller goes out

First Storyteller There is no fairground scene in . . .
Producer Now listen to me! (*He builds his speech into a towering rage. He points to the First Storyteller*) I'm not having this. You walked out! You couldn't be found. Because you walked out I cancelled your play. One out—all out: Union rules. Your play will remain cancelled. And there is no room for you in the new play. Do you hear? If you think you are going to spoil people's enjoyment, you are mistaken. This is where you get off and we get on with it. This is where you get off so that we can get on with it. Do you hear? Now get off! Get off! Get off! Get off! Get off!
First Storyteller But you can't just do that. We've been to all the re-hearsals. We all know our parts. We've learned our lines.
Pyramus This is an old tale . . .

The Producer brings out a whistle which he blows fiercely, and points to the back of the auditorium

Producer Get off!
Thisbe But what about our costumes . . .
Producer Off! Go on. Off.

The First Storyteller, Pyramus, and Thisbe crowd round the Producer. They jostle and argue, but the Producer remains firm. He takes Thisbe's name. Eventually they leave down the aisle C, *muttering*

First Storyteller (*from the back of the auditorium*) We'll be at the fairground, anyway. We'll be waiting for you.
Thisbe (*as they go out*) But there is no fairground scene in our play.

The First Storyteller, Pyramus and Thisbe leave

The Producer turns to the audience

Producer I am sorry about that. I hope you weren't too upset by it all. I don't like making a scene. It's their own fault, of course. We can manage without them. I shall call the new play *The Legend of Orpheus*. Yes. A good title, that. Straight to the point. (*He looks into the wings*) We're ready now, I think. I'll just check. (*Calling*) Merry-go-round ready?

The first few bars of the "Carousel Waltz" blare out through the loudspeakers

Steamboat ready?

A very loud hiss of steam, and then the sound of an over-full whistling kettle coming to the boil

Barrel-organ ready?

A loud popping noise followed by a long gurgling sound. Then a voice singing drunkenly, "You Are My Sunshine"

Roller-Coaster ready?

Silence

Roller-Coaster ready?

The Second Storyteller appears

Second Storyteller It's broken.
Producer What?
Second Storyteller It's broken.
Producer But it can't be. The cast has got to ride in it.
Second Storyteller Well, it is. Harry says the cam shaft's gone. You could just use sound effects though. Sort of pretend like.
Producer Oh this is too bad. This was to be the greatest scene staged on the English scene, seen on the English stage. I had it all planned out. It was going to go: bubububur bububur bubur tick tick tick tick tick tick tick tick tick tick tick tick tick ticktick tick tick ticktick ticktick ticktick tickticktickticktick mmmmmmmmmmmmmmmmmmooooooooooooooooo oooooooooooooooommmmmmmmmmmmmmmmmmmmmmmmmmmmmm mmeeeeeeeeeeeeeeeeeeeeeeeeeeeeeewwwwwwwwwwwwwwwwwwwwwww ww tick tick tick tick ticktickticktickmmmmmmmmmmmmmmmmmmmm

mmmmmooooooooooooooooooooooooommmmmmmmmmmmmmmmmm
mmmmmooooooooooooooooooooooooommmmmmmmmmmmmmmmmm
wwwwwwwwwwwww. And now it's broken?

Second Storyteller Broken! (*Tonelessly*) Broken!

Harry, the Technician, enters

Harry There's a gentleman 'ere by the name of Mr Aristaeus. Rather peculiar. He's got a uniform on like he was a bee-keeper. Says he mends Roller-Coasters and believes you're 'aving a spot of trouble with yours.

The Producer and Second Storyteller look at each other. The Producer offers a quiet prayer

Producer (*to the Second Storyteller*) After you.

Second Storyteller No, after you. (*He bows*)

They both wait, and then both make a dash for it. Harry follows, shaking his head

SCENE 5

Eurydice comes in with the Wood Nymphs and Woodland Animals

Song: "MY HOME IS THE FOREST"

Eurydice ⎤ (*singing*)
Wood Nymphs ⎱ My home is the forest, the valley and the hills,
Woodland ⎰ Where the clear stream gushes in a thousand dainty rills;
Animals ⎦ Can I leave it all, every tree and leaf,
And go to the town to spend my life?

Every lily of the valley, and every owl that's wise,
Tell me that I would be foolish to leave this paradise;
Hill, dell, twig, leaf, all tell me that I'd grieve,
If I left the forest, I'd find strife.

First Wood Nymph But if you love Orpheus, you must go.

Second Wood Nymph How could you stay here?

Third Wood Nymph You'd soon get used to it.

Eurydice Oh, I don't know what to do.

First Wood Nymph Go with him.

Second Wood Nymph Be happy.

Third Wood Nymph It would be nice to have a mortal as a brother-in-law.

Wood Nymphs ⎤ (*singing*)
Woodland ⎱ Your home was the forest, the valley, and the hills,
Animals ⎦ Where the clear stream gushes in a thousand dainty rills,

> But you must leave it all, every tree and leaf,
> And go to the town to be his wife!

They break off, laughing

Orpheus comes in

First Wood Nymph Orpheus! She'll go with you.
Eurydice I'll try . . .
Second Wood Nymph We know you'll be happy.
Orpheus There's a fair in the village.
Third Wood Nymph A fair!
Orpheus Eurydice, let's go to the fair. It will be as happy a time as you could wish for!
Eurydice I'm still afraid. There was a warning when you were last here.
Orpheus It's nothing.
Eurydice I know it means me.
Orpheus But what harm is there at a fair?
Eurydice I don't know.
Orpheus Come on, then. We'll have a good time. Come on, smile!

Orpheus takes her hand. Eurydice relents, smiles, and they go out. The Wood Nymphs and Woodland Animals cheer and dance after them

SCENE 6

A gong sounds. The stage is flooded with colourful light. There is a great burst of noise, laughter, and shouting. People flock to the fair. Music, dancing, gaiety. Stalls are set up by various showmen and their assistants. The entrance to the Roller-Coaster is set up on stage. People with paper hats and balloons are milling up and down the centre aisle as a general dance and song takes place on stage

Song: "ALL THE FUN OF THE FAIR"

Crowd All the fun of the fair, the fair
All the fun . . .
The fair, the fair, the fair, the fair,
The fair, the fun of the fair.

The fair, the fun of the fair, the fair,
All the fun of the fair,
The fun of the fair, the fun of the fair.

The fair, the fun of the fair,
The fun of the fair, the fun of the fair

The fun of the fair, the fun of the fun
Of the fun of the fair. Hey! Hey!

They break off, cheering and laughing, and mingle with the crowd

*Acrobats, fire-eaters, magicians enter. After a moment Orpheus and
Eurydice come in*

Orpheus They won't hurt you. They're only having fun.
Eurydice They frighten me.
Orpheus But they won't hurt. This is holiday time. You'll soon get used
to it. It may be noisier than living in the wood, but that's all. Come on,
let's see what's over there.
Eurydice Oh, Orpheus, please take me away.

They mingle with the crowd

*The First Storyteller, Pyramus and Thisbe enter. The Second Storyteller,
in showman's costume, follows, and gets ready to open his booth*

*The music and activity gradually dies away as the Showmen start to shout
their wares. The crowd stands listening*

Eurydice I'm sorry, Orpheus, but there are too many people. I miss the
peacefulness of my tree-home.

Before Orpheus can reply the Second Storyteller beats his drum

Second Storyteller Roll up! Roll up! The Greatest Show on Earth!

All the Showmen start shouting in rotation

First Showman Come along now please—only five pence for the Bye-
Cy-cerling Rat!
Second Showman The Only Living Badger with a Yooman 'Ead!
Third Showman Incredible as it may seem, before your very eyes he will
climb up this rope and disappear. From the magic lands of the East,
hidden in the mists of time . . .
Fourth Showman You won't believe it! The Boxing Bear versus Grappling
Joe Gresty of Borneo! A Fight to the Finish! And to you not twenty
pence, not even ten pence, but five pence! Five pence . . .
Second Storyteller Roll up! Roll up!
First Showman The value's there folks!
Fifth Showman Just step right this way! The Living Mummy! And the
one hundredth customer gets a jewelled casket clustered with Nubian
pearls. Only five pence! Five penny-worth of the finest value you can
buy . . .
Sixth Showman Have you seen The Lizard Woman? Brought to you at
great expense and for the first time. All the way from the Amazon
swamps. Release the grip on those sticky little pennies, clenched in your
hot little hands. It's feeding time! Hurry, hurry!

The Second Storyteller beats his bass drum and gradually draws the crowd's attention from the other Showmen

Second Storyteller See Madam Carlotta de Venezuela, the great South American Giantess! So enormous that a special ship had to be made to bring her 'ere! For your vital information she measures: sixteen-and-a-half yards round the waist . . .

Crowd Ooooooooooooh!

Second Storyteller Three feet four-and-a-quarter inches round the ankle . . .

Crowd Aaaaaaaaaaah!

Second Storyteller Weighs nine tons and stands seventeen feet three inches in her stocking feet!

Crowd Cor! Hurray! Whooooo! She's big! etc.

Some of the crowd pay and go into the Second Storyteller's booth

Thisbe I think I'd like to see that fat woman, Pyramus. I say, Mister, how much is it?

Second Storyteller Only five pence, just about to begin!

Thisbe Aye, come on Pyramus, you can afford it. (*To the First Storyteller*) Are you coming with us?

First Storyteller Well, yes. (*To the audience*) I'll find a way to get into this new play, and in doing so, further my revenge!

Pyramus, Thisbe and the First Storyteller go into the booth

Orpheus and Eurydice come forward. Orpheus is trying to console her. The crowd remaining gathers round

Orpheus Listen, Eurydice, they won't harm you. They are only people. It's strange at first . . .

Eurydice But there's no peace here, not like the woodland. So many, such a noise.

First Villager What have you got there, Orpheus? Is it a Wood Nymph?

Second Villager What's he doing with a Wood Nymph, then?

Third Villager Going to set up his own side-show, I shouldn't wonder!

The crowd laughs

First Villager Come on, Orpheus, let's have a look at her.

Fourth Villager We'll tell you if she's worth a bob or two.

Third Villager Aye, come on. It's not every day you see a Wood Nymph. I've been trying to catch one for years!

The Villagers press round, clamouring and trying to see Eurydice, who is extremely frightened and hides her face on Orpheus's shoulder

Second Villager Come on, chuck, let's have a look at you.

First Villager Come on. Don't be shy.

The Second Villager takes hold of Eurydice's hair and tries to pull her face away from Orpheus's shoulder

Orpheus Get away! Get away from her!

Orpheus sweeps at the Second Villager, who springs back in alarm

First Villager Now don't be mean now. We only . . .
Orpheus I mean it. Get away. Get back, and leave us alone.
Second Villager Very possessive, isn't he?
Fourth Villager Oh come on. He's not in a very good humour today.
Orpheus Just leave us alone.
Third Villager (*with mock civility*) Yes, sir! Of course, sir! Anything you say, sir! (*He bows low*)
First Villager It's a poor show if you can't take a joke.
Fourth Villager Oh, come on everybody. Let's go and see the Living Mummy.
Second Villager Now there's something really worth looking at!

The Villagers disperse with grumbles. A chorus of "Ee-ay-addio, He Wants to be Alone" puts them in better humour

Orpheus and Eurydice are left alone. Eurydice is weeping quietly. Pause

Orpheus I'm sorry.
Eurydice It's all right.
Orpheus They only meant it as a joke. What can I say? You wouldn't understand. I've made a mess of things.
Eurydice Oh, Orpheus, I can't stay here. I shall go mad and die, I know it.

Pause

Orpheus We'll go back to the woodland. If that will make you happy, we'll go back there, to the big trees and the green light.
Eurydice Oh yes, oh yes.
Orpheus And there we'll smile, and the forest will echo with singing. I'll make you a crown of leaves, and a tambourine, and you shall be Queen of the Greenwood.
Eurydice Yes, yes.
Orpheus Come on, then, no tears. Don't be upset. We'll go back to the forest.

Before Orpheus and Eurydice can depart there is a great shout and the crowd comes pouring out of the Second Storyteller's booth. The First Storyteller, Pyramus, and Thisbe emerge at the head of the column of Villagers

First Storyteller That fat woman is rubbish! Rubbish!
Thisbe It's a swindle!

Exclamations and nods of agreement from the crowd

Second Storyteller You're not supposed to be in this play, anyway, so don't you go putting them off or I'll have you in court for slander. And sabotage.

Thisbe I'll not spend a penny in there again!

Second Storyteller Now just you pipe down, you tattered old rag-bag!

Pyramus Now look 'ere . . .

Second Storyteller You clear off from here, you dim-witted loon, I'm sick of you, and—(*pointing to Thisbe*)—take that grisly horror with you—before I get annoyed!

Pyramus Did you hear that? Did you hear that? (*He points at Thisbe and addresses the Second Storyteller*) That's my finance, you brainless buffoon, that's my finance.

Second Storyteller Oh you poor wretch—engaged to that! (*To Thisbe*) You grasshopper. You wet fish.

Pyramus Now look 'ere. Look 'ere.

Thisbe You give us our money back, you thieving parrot!

First Storyteller Pierrot.

Thisbe Pierrot.

Second Storyteller I told you to get lost, you rickety old windbag. Now go on—clear off.

Pyramus Enough! Eeeeeeeeeeeeeeeeeeeeeeeeeenuff! I'm going to paste you.

The Second Storyteller turns away scornfully. Pyramus rolls up his sleeves

Pyramus I am going to box the big red ears on your tiny head.

The Second Storyteller suddenly turns and roars like a lion. Pyramus is very frightened, and jumps back in alarm

Now be warned! (*He backs away, ducking and weaving*) I'll put your lamps out!

Pyramus backs further as the Second Storyteller advances, and trips backwards over a tent peg. He gets up very quickly

(*With a last show of bravado*) Watch it! Watch it!

Second Storyteller Come on then, come on.

Pyramus backs into a line of Villagers closing in, and can back-pedal no more. The Villagers make no attempt to hold him

Pyramus Let me get at him! Stop holding me back!

Thisbe Go on Pyramus: make a pie of 'im!

Pyramus Yes, I will—but my sore arm . . .

Thisbe runs round behind the Second Storyteller, kicks his bottom, and sends him sprawling forward. At the same time the Villagers push the reluctant Pyramus forward into the Second Storyteller's arms. The crowd rings round the fighters, hiding them from view and shouting encouragement. Thisbe races round the outside of the ring trying to see what is happening

Thisbe (*bellowing above the noise of the Crowd*) Go on, Pyramus! Maim 'im, Pyramus! Kick his teeth down his throat! Oh, maim 'im.

At the height of the mêlée the sound of the Roller-Coaster begins to click through the loudspeakers. The fight breaks off as the noise of the Roller-Coaster increases

Crowd Listen! It's the Roller-Coaster! They've mended it! They've mended it! They've got it working! They've got it working at last! Great! Come on! Let's have a ride! Come on, the Roller-Coaster's working. The Roller-Coaster, the Roller-Coaster, etc., *ad lib.*

The scene is one of confusion as the Crowd goes wild and streams off in the direction of the Roller-Coaster

The noise of the Roller-Coaster increases. Eurydice is frightened out of her wits. She gesticulates wildly, flinging out her arms and covering her face and ears

Eurydice Oh, Orpheus, it's frightening me to death! I can't stand it! Let me go, let me go, let me go! (*She pushes her way through the Crowd milling on stage. She covers her face as she runs backstage*)
Orpheus (*trying to push his way through the mass*) Eurydice! Eurydice! Eurydice! Wait. Wait. Wait! Wait for me. Eurydice, wait for me! There's nothing to fear! Wait, wait!

SCENE 7

Thunder and lightning. The stage darkens. The wind howls. Stalls and crowd have disappeared

Eurydice appears in the forest. She is still panic-stricken and runs wildly in all directions. The storm frightens her further. In her blind running she steps on a snake which strikes at her ankles

Eurydice Oh, a snake, a snake! (*She draws back in horror*) A cobra! Oh, no, a cobra. I shall die! (*She sits down and nurses her ankle. Muttering to herself*) Oh, Orpheus—a cobra, a cobra. (*She weeps, tries to stand, can't, tries to drag herself along the ground. Her movements turn from the frantic to slow, painful efforts*) Orpheus, Orpheus . . . (*Finally, she lies still*)

The storm dies away. Pause

From the shadows emerge four weird figures, dressed in black. They are Mourners from the Underworld. They stand watching over Eurydice stand watching over Eurydice

A loud whisper echoes through the loudspeakers

Voice Bring her down to the Shadows. Bring her into the Gloom.

Quiet but foreboding music. The four figures cast their spell. Eurydice rises, entranced. The Mourners put black lace over her face, surround her, and walk with her slowly down the aisle C. *They are joined by five more Underworld figures. The procession moves out silently to solemn music*

SCENE 8

Dawn. The stage lights brighten a little

One or two Woodland Animals creep in and sit quietly. A bird can be heard singing. Orpheus, weary with fatigue, comes in slowly

Orpheus Eurydice!

There is no answer. Only the birds are singing

Eurydice! (*He sees one of the Woodland Animals*) Have you seen her?

The Animal points down R. *Orpheus hurries down to the Animal positioned at the entrance to the aisle* L

Have you seen her?

The Animal shakes its head, and turns away. Orpheus hurries to the Animal guarding the aisle C

Have you seen her?

The Animal points to the back of the auditorium

This way? Down here?

The Animal points again down aisle C, *and then moves slowly away. All the Woodland Animals now retreat slowly with heads bowed. Orpheus looks round despairingly*

Eurydice!

There is still no answer. He starts to hurry down the aisle C, *and breaks into a stumbling run*

Eurydice! Eurydice!

Orpheus disappears into the entrance hall. His voice can be heard echoing

Eurydice! Eurydice!

His last cry is one of utter desperation

The song of the birds fades. The Stage Lights dim out

The House Lights come up for the end of Act I

ACT II

Scene 1

L of the stage is a flight of steps; R are two levels separated by a gap through which stairs can be seen going down. An entrance way C is curtained off by black drapes. Above this entrance is a platform holding a stone which is crudely fashioned in the shape of a throne. This area is completely blacked out when the Act starts

At first there is only a faint light directed on to the apron, as Orpheus comes in, but this light grows brighter during the scene, to reflect the harshness of winter and to suggest the passing of time

Orpheus enters L

Song: "BLUEBELLS"

Orpheus Blue, blue, blue bluebells
        Dying in the gloomy wood,
        And grey, grey, grey turns the wintry sea;
        Black and cold are the hollow hazel shells,
        And pale the hand that beckons me

        Dark, dark, dark death spells
        Its peril on the frost-bound bud,
        And gone, gone, gone is Eurydice;
        Alone, alone, my voice echoes through the dells,
        Where, where is she?
        Where is she?

He sits down and stares into the distance

The light on him dims, and a fiercely bright light comes up on the Third Storyteller. Unlike the other two Storytellers this one has a grim, purposeful appearance. He is dressed in black with a black hood and a very white face with thin red lips. He could be Death or Fate, but at any rate his appearance should be mysterious

Third Storyteller All that summer, and through the autumn and winter which gripped the earth, Orpheus searched. His search took him up into stony mountains, where eagles cry, and through deep, enchanted woods full of wings and strange murmurings. Without success. He searched the rivers and fields. Without success. In lonely places, where the only sign of life is a wall or a few sheep, he questioned farmers or the odd traveller on some little used road. They shook their heads. Eurydice was nowhere to be found. (*Pause. He moves downstage*) When spring returns, with its feeling of being born again, not for Orpheus will there be the pleasure of new leaves, of new life shooting out of the soil. Look at him—disconsolate, forlorn, worn out by his long search. All he can do now is ponder on the happiness he had. The gods gave him little enough. (*He pauses*)

But basically the gods are kind. They intrude upon our lives at important points, make changes—for good or ill—impose conditions, deprive. They are like parents, perhaps. Poor Orpheus! The gods have not punished him because he did anything wrong, but because it was his misfortune to fall in love with a Wood Nymph. He mistook the dream for reality. How could he hope to capture and keep such a creature—a being whose very spirit was of the trees and air; light, and delicate as a leaf! She could never survive in the modern world! He won't give in, you know, won't settle for anything less. It has to be Eurydice. Expensive clothes, perfumes, painted finger-nails make no impression on him. He's rather stubborn, isn't he? He still has the pride of the soldier. His idealism is so inflexible. But the odds are stacked against him. He's bound to suffer. Will he be better for it? Well, the gods think so. I was with them during the interval, when you were drinking tea or lemonade and eating your sweets and biscuits, and this is their considered opinion. They think suffering "improves" a man. And into his dream I have to fit the nightmare, tell him the truth—what he has long suspected in his hearts of hearts. (*He turns and addresses Orpheus coldly*) Orpheus, Orpheus, listen. Learn this: Eurydice is dead, Orpheus. Eurydice is dead. Struck at by the cobra, her body lies cold, entombed in the Land of Shadows. If you dare go into that dark place, seek her there. You will be shown the way. Follow the Mourners of the King of the Shadows. If you dare go—or forget her.

The Third Storyteller vanishes into the shadows

Orpheus wakes. Pause

Orpheus Dead? I dreamed she was dead. It can't be. (*A long pause*) It is true. I know it. Dead. Dead.

Pause

A black funeral procession winds its solemn way across the stage, singing. It consists of nine Mourners with Eurydice, veiled

Mourners Down, down, down, down, into the depths,
     The dark, where Hades reigns and the Shadows sigh,
     Into the dark, deep down, where the long-dead lie.
Orpheus She has faded into the Realm of the Silent where Hades rules. All her bloom veiled, shrouded, by non-living shadows. (*He turns and watches the Mourners*) And they go that way. Oh, what horror lurks there! No man can tell. What claws, what icy, shivering fingers of

ghouls strangle and grip! What morbid mouths whisper! What agony!
(*Pause*) I will seek this Dark King of Death. I have endured many
bitter times: on Jason's voyage for the Golden Fleece we still believed
that deeds of daring and unflinching courage were worthy of men's
praise. But this dark journey has more dread than any snatching of a
Fleece from the Gorgon's cold stare.

Orpheus calls to the Mourners, who are disappearing down the steps

Lead on, you who know better than any, where death lies. I'll find
Eurydice in that mournful land. Lead on.

Orpheus goes after the Mourners and the veiled Eurydice

SCENE 2

The lights brighten on stage

*Six Mourners file on to the stage, among them the First Storyteller, Pyramus,
and Thisbe. The Second Storyteller comes in*

Second Storyteller Into line quickly. Come on, hurry. Mourners! Mourners . . . Attention! Dressing! Right—Dress! Eyes . . . Front! Stand at—
Ease! Mourners . . . Attention! As you were! You're not awake today,
are you? Now wait for it. Mourners . . . Attention!

The Producer comes in. He wears a military cap and carries an officer's cane

Mourners all present and ready for your inspection, *sir*!
Producer (*with a Sandhurst accent*) Thank you, Mr Storyteller. (*He walks
slowly down the line of Mourners, inspecting them*) Do your button up,
laddie. That's better. (*He stops at Pyramus*) Do you usually mourn in
these clothes, Mourner?
Pyramus Well, I didn't really have time to change. You see, I had a
different part . . .
Producer Mr Storyteller. Take this man's name.
Second Storyteller Sir!

The Producer stops at Thisbe

Producer What's this?
Second Storyteller Mourner Thisbe, sir. Co-opted from the Special
Effects Department—by the—er—by the Technician, sir.
Producer Tell the Technician I want to see him, will you?
Second Storyteller Sir!

The Second Storyteller marches out

The Producer reaches the First Storyteller

Producer Well turned out. Very well turned out. Perhaps a little more sorrow on the face, but generally very good.

First Storyteller Thank you, sir.

Producer Haven't I seen you somewhere before?

First Storyteller Well, I've been all sorts of things in my time, sir.

Producer Hmmm. Well now, listen you people. Your part in this play will require the utmost delicacy and tact. We've had to make a lot of changes for one reason or another, and we don't want a tragedy on our hands. It is now twenty forty-five hours, and after this briefing your main job will be The Consolation of Orpheus. You are Sympathisers, got it? You will sing to him, bring him round, make him feel that his loss is not as bad as all that. If you do your job well, we should have him back on his own two feet by twenty-one thirty hours, and we can end happily.

The Second Storyteller enters with Harry, the Technician

Now, are there any . . . . Ah. Come here, Technician. (*He points to Thisbe*) What's the meaning of this?

Harry What?

Producer This. This—heap!

Harry Oh, that. Well, it was very short notice you understand. But she was to be one of the Mourners, sir.

Producer Yes, I know that. But her dress, man, her dress.

Harry Costumes didn't have no trousers, sir.

Producer I'm not bothered about trousers. At least, er—what I mean to say is . . . The fact is, Technician, that she is improperly dressed for mourning.

Harry I don't see that matters now, sir. Not now that the Mourners have gone, sir, if you see what I mean.

Producer The Mourners have gone?

Harry Yes, sir.

Producer The Mourners have gone, Technician?

Harry Yes, sir. That's right, sir.

Producer (*slowly, determined to reduce the Technician to ashes with his biting scorn*) Well, if the Mourners have gone, Technician, what are these people doing here? Who am I inspecting? And why am I inspecting them?

Harry Oh, well, they were to be Mourners, sir, I quite agree, but when you sent that other lot . . .

Producer I sent "that other lot"?

Harry Yes sir. When you sent that other lot, "Harry," I said to myself— that's my name, sir—Harry—"Harry," I said to myself, "them's real character actors." That lot in black, and all singing! All dark, creepy and mysterious-like! You'd have thought they were from Hell itself, sir.

Producer Quite, quite. Yes. Well. (*To the audience, nervous and apprehensive*) I didn't send them! Something—can't—have—happened?
Harry So naturally I didn't bother when Orpheus went after them.
Producer (*turning pale*) You didn't—bother?
Harry No, sir.
Producer You didn't bother, when Orpheus went after them?
Harry That's right, sir.
Producer I see.
Harry I mean, it's only pretend like, isn't it?
Producer (*gulping*) Ha? Oh, yes, of course, of course. Ah!
Harry Will that be all, sir?
Producer I'm afraid it will, Technician. I'm afraid it will.

The Second Storyteller marches the Mourners and Harry the Technician out

"Angels and ministers of grace defend us!" I didn't send those Mourners. The fool! He's gone. Down—there! Oh misery! They'll send me to prison! To prison! (*He stands visibly trembling*)

Mrs Hawkins comes down the aisle c

Mrs Hawkins Here, you.
Producer Oh! Oh how nice to see you, how very nice!
Mrs Hawkins What have you done with my boy?
Producer Orpheus, you mean? Well, erm, it's rather difficult to explain, actually. Nothing to worry about you understand. But—erm . . .
Mrs Hawkins You borrowed my boy. What have you done with him?
Producer Well, you see—I'm afraid there's been a technical hitch.
Mrs Hawkins A technical hitch?
Producer Now it wasn't intentional. Please understand that. There was nothing intentional about it. I had nothing against him. He was quite a nice boy, really. I do hope there won't be any hard feelings . . .

The Producer backs away as Mrs Hawkins advances on to the stage. He is almost hysterical with fright

The fact is—he's gone. He's departed. A dreadful mistake. I'm very sorry about it. Hell can be quite nice at this time of year. But I'm sure he'll come back, eventually.

He turns and flees, roaring at the top of his voice, as Mrs Hawkins chases him

Perhaps even before the play is over. If you'll just be patient . . .

The Producer and Mrs Hawkins disappear into the wings

There is a terrific crash, a low moan, and then silence. The Lights dim on stage

SCENE 3

Foreboding music is heard

A faint light appears on the shadows of the Mourners as they escort Eurydice across the stage. Their voices echo as they whisper their song

Song: "DOWN, DOWN INTO THE DEPTHS"

Mourners (*singing*)
>   Down, down, down, down, into the depths,
>   The dark, where Hades reigns and the Shadows sigh
>   Into the dark, deep down, into the dark, deep down, where the
>   long-dead lie.
>
>   Down, down, down, down, into the depths,
>   The dark, where dreams are pains and the tortured cry,
>   Into the dark, deep down,
>   Into the dark, deep down, where lives drain and die.

Orpheus appears at the top of the steps. He starts to descend slowly, fearfully. The Mourners disappear. Their murmuring fades away. Silence

Orpheus Cold, cold.

A figure appears at the bottom of the steps. It is immensely old, tattered, and haggard

There is the sound of water lapping

No hideous nightmare could conjure this. The mouth of Hell! How many souls have passed this way, distressed, lost to Time and all remembrance! (*He reaches the bottom step, but does not see the figure of Charon until it speaks to him*)

Charon By what permission do you step this deadly way?

Orpheus A sign from the gods. I dreamed Eurydice was dead.

Charon We have few living visitors. I am Charon, the Ferryman of the Dead. If you wish to pass across these black waters you must pay the fee. My boats wait. Will you pay the fee? A coin for the eyes of the dead?

Orpheus I will.

Charon This way, then.

They move L

Cerberus will not harm you if you are expected. But there are other dangers. This way.

Charon and Orpheus go out. Weird forms appear and group themselves on the steps and levels

A skull flashes in the black light. There are low groans, then silence

Orpheus appears with Charon at the top of the steps

Down there! Be careful. I should not like to think the Ferry of the Dead has lost a good customer. No doubt we'll meet again—when the time comes!

Charon goes away, leaving Orpheus alone

Orpheus descends the steps through an avenue of shapes which seek to grasp him, and which whisper hatefully. A mime and ballet of the dead, using black light and luminous paint, follows

Orpheus Oh monstrous world. Monstrous, monstrous.

A red glow. Groans, shrieks, wailing yells reverberate through the auditorium. Orpheus reaches the bottom step

Foul, rank.

The Third Storyteller, carrying a lantern, enters and waits on the steps of the apron

It's like some evil dream, hideous, unnatural. I have not the words to speak of it.

Third Storyteller Orpheus, come.

Orpheus sees him for the first time

Come. This way. I am here to guide you.

Orpheus joins him and they cross the steps together

Judge not too harshly, Orpheus. You have just come through the Punishment Chambers. There is not far to go.

Orpheus Is that where Ixion was bound upon the wheel?

Third Storyteller Indeed yes, and many other demons and pitiless creatures pay their penalty here in fire, chains and torment. But we have more pleasant pastimes for those who were noble in their lives.

Orpheus Where is Eurydice?

Third Storyteller All in good time. This way. She feels no pain, if that is what you mean. No pain.

Orpheus Will Hades let her go?

Third Storyteller That depends. But Hades is merciful, even kind, to those who deserve mercy.

A blood-curdling howling echoes through the loudspeakers

Cerberus—the dog of Hell—dealing with some malignant spirit. You are wise to be afraid. The gods might think you were too proud to show your fear. That would incur their wrath. They would not hesitate.

Orpheus Who, then, are you, that know their scheming?

Third Storyteller Ah, we are nearly there. The last flight of steps.

Orpheus and the Third Storyteller go out

SCENE 4

The Great Hall of Hades' Kingdom

Hades sits on his high throne above the entrance way with Persephone, his pale-faced queen. In the dim light weird figures can be seen performing a ritualistic dance. Several guards hold banners with strange inscriptions. Minos, Rhadamanthus, and Aeacus, the Judges of the Underworld, sit on lesser thrones on the lower levels

The Mourners enter with Eurydice

Song: "DOWN, DOWN INTO THE DEPTHS" (Reprise)

Mourners (*singing*)
 Down, down, down, down, into the depths,
 The dark, where Hades reigns and the Shadows sigh,
 Into the dark, deep down, where the flames rise high.

 Down, down, down, down, into the depths,
 The dark, where black night stains the echoing sky,
 Into the dark, deep down, where the long-dead lie.

The Mourners group themselves round Eurydice

Minos, Rhadamanthus, and Aeacus pronounce judgement on a Spirit that is brought weeping before them

Minos Since no-one comes to plead your cause: hear our sentence! You are convicted of murder most foul. Foul poisoner, the slaughter of that Innocent will lie heavy on your soul. (*Raising his voice*) You will be bound to The Wheel of Fire to cleanse your evil spirit, and thence cast into The Pit of Serpents for all eternity.

Rhadamanthus (*intoning*) The Pit of Serpents.

Aecus (*intoning*) For all eternity.

The Great Hall echoes as they hammer their wooden mallets

Spirit Oh no. No, no, no.

The Spirit is borne out by two guards, shrieking. A second Spirit is brought in

Rhadamanthus We have weighed the evidence brought to us by your witnesses. They lie!

Aeacus They lie!

Minos They lie!

Rhadamanthus Hear our just sentence upon you for your abominable crime! You will be put into The Cage of Pestilence where the rats gnaw at your ears and eyes. For ever!

Minos
Aeacus } *(shouting)* For ever! { *(Speaking together)*

The Second Spirit is hustled away, pleading for mercy

Hades Bring Eurydice before us!

Eurydice steps forward. Her veil is lifted from her by one of the Mourners. The Three Judges lay down their wooden mallets

Minos Who will plead for the Wood Nymph?

Silence

Rhadamanthus Who pleads for Eurydice?

Silence

Aeacus Who pleads her cause?

The Third Storyteller and Orpheus enter

Third Storyteller My lord!

Hades Wait. Who comes? Let him approach.

Third Storyteller Your servant, great King, with Orpheus.

Hades Upon what errand?

Orpheus I come to plead with the great King and Judges of the Underworld for the life of Eurydice, the Wood Nymph.

The Judges confer

Hades The living of this Nymph had virtue in it. Upon what justification do you plead?

Third Storyteller He is deeply in love with her, my lord.

Hades We may dispute that. There is no deeper love within these walls than mine for Queen Persephone. How much of his is just mere childish game and sport of youth?

The Judges again confer

Orpheus The fact that I have dared your wrath, my lord, to come within this dreadful place of judgement, is surely testimony of my love.

Minos My lord, we are agreed that since her spirit shows no unnatural taint she need not be detained in purgatory. We welcome your advice.

Rhadamanthus It is a most unusual case, my lord, when a mortal comes to plead for the dead.

Hades It shows courage, too!

Persephone (*sadly, as if thinking of herself*) Let her go, my lord. She has done no harm. She is only young.

Hades (*after deliberation*) Well, Orpheus, for your courage in journeying to these Shades, where festered minds pay for the suffering they have caused, we decree that Eurydice may go from here. (*Pause*) Let her, unfettered, roam our Elysian fields: her spirit will find woods to play in. When she has sipped the waters of oblivion, she will find happiness. Bear her away!

As The Guards step forward Orpheus realizes that it is not the intention to release Eurydice

Orpheus My lord, you reward my courage, but my journey was made for love. I beg you to restore Eurydice to her former life, that I may take her hence to find true happiness on earth.

Aeacus It cannot be!

Hades Don't be too hasty, Aeacus. I shall be the judge of this. Beware of your pride! If we grant this favour, Orpheus, what will you give in return?

Orpheus I have nothing to give, my lord. My gratitude, my music in your praise.

Song: "O SPIRIT OF DEATH"

(*Singing*) O spirit of death, how cold is her brow,
But 'tis her that I love, for ever I know.

O spirit of life, give back once again
My love to the fields, the hills, and the rain.

O spirit of life, spirit of death,
Restore her to me, and to the green earth.

Hades confers with Persephone

Hades Enough, then. She shall be yours.

Orpheus My lord . . .

Hades Upon condition.

Orpheus My lord?

Hades We require some further token of your faith in her and of your duty to us. We release Eurydice upon condition that in going hence you look not back on her. You must have faith that she will be following.

Orpheus My lord, I will not look back. I will have faith.

Hades Should you look back we will reclaim her soul for ever, as forfeit for your disobedience and lack of faith in us.

Orpheus I will not fail. I put my trust in you, great king.

Hades Restore Eurydice to her sweet bloom of youth!

Music and mime, during which Eurydice awakens as if from a deep sleep

Go, Orpheus. Remember: look back and she is lost to you.

Orpheus bows, turns, and walks slowly away

Follow him, Eurydice. He has endured many dangers for the love of thee. Such a one deserves thy love. Let it be known that I have shown mercy.

Eurydice I will, my lord. (*She kneels, rises, turns, and slowly follows Orpheus at some little distance*)

Hades Come, Persephone, and attendant lords. We will escort them to our Upper Halls and mark their progress. Come.

The procession moves out

The Stage Lights dim

SCENE 5

The Stage Lights come up again

The Producer enters, with the Second Storyteller, and Harry, the Technician

Producer But what am I going to do? Supposing he doesn't come back? I can't just say, "Oh, her son has gone to Hell," as if he'd gone on a cruise or something. The police won't stand for that.

Second Storyteller It seems to me you're taking this far too seriously. It's only a play, you know.

Producer It *was* a play. Won't you realize that? Was. Was. But it's happened! It was those Mourners! It's gone real! Now it's entirely out of my hands! (*To the Technician*) If only you'd had the sense not to let that crowd of demons on to the stage, everything would have been all right. We'd have all gone home by now.

Harry Oh charming! Perfectly charming! All this is my fault. Mend a fuse here and there and you cop for the lot! Let me remind you that casting is your problem, not mine. I'm paid for fuses, sound effects, and sweeping up.

Producer Oh, typical! You know your rights don't you? You know which side your bread is buttered!

Harry I'm just not putting my name to no manslaughter charge, that's all.

Producer Ah, yes. It's at times like this one finds who one's friends are!

Harry Can I help it if you can't distinguish between natural and super-natural?

Producer That's right. Blame it *all* on me. Go on! The fact that I never set eyes on *your* Mourners has nothing whatever to do with it. It's my fault, of course, that *you* let them on stage.

Second Storyteller Look, it seems to me . . .

Producer Oh it does, does it? Well, don't you start. Just you keep out of this!

Second Storyteller I only said . . .

Producer You only messed things up right at the beginning. If it wasn't for you, none of this would have happened. You were supposed to look after the machines.

Harry (*in emphatic agreement*) Yes, he was.

Second Storyteller Now wait a minute!

Producer Instead you cause my narrator to walk out, you beat up my male lead . . .

Second Storyteller That was Pyramus in the other play . . .

Producer I don't care which play it was in. You beat him up!

Second Storyteller He was trying to damage the plot.

Producer Damage the plot! Damage the plot! Did you hear that?

Harry He was trying to damage the plot!

Producer Well, that's just marvellous. Marvellous. That's made my day, that has. Would you be so kind as to tell us, Mr Dramatic Critic, exactly which plot he was trying to damage?

Second Storyteller (*confused*) Well—er—I don't know.

Harry He doesn't know!

Producer He doesn't know.

While the Producer is speaking, Pyramus, Thisbe and the First Storyteller come on

(*To the audience*) There speaks a man of wisdom, a man supposed to know a lot about electronics.

The Second Storyteller bursts into tears and runs off stage

When the Producer turns round he finds himself addressing Thisbe

You gormless heap! You complicated moron! You prize wretch! You cabbage! You nauseating, ugly, distorted . . . Oh.

Pyramus Don't you talk to my finance like that. You're no oil painting either!

Thisbe Very polite, I'm sure.

Thisbe suddenly grabs the Producer by the neck and with a great shout of "Whaa" brings him smartly to the canvas with a perfect karate blow

Pyramus Perhaps that'll teach you to be more careful with the compliments.

Producer (*getting up slowly and painfully*) I didn't mean her, you great oaf!

Thisbe takes a pace forward

(*Shouting at the top of his voice*) No, now let's be reasonable. Let's all keep calm.

First Storyteller You promised us jobs as Mourners. You ought to learn to keep your promises.

Producer I didn't—that is . . . The fact is that things have got rather out of control.

Thisbe We were supposed to be the stars of this play. You said so.
Producer I didn't.
Thisbe You did.
Producer I didn't.
Thisbe Oh yes you did.
Producer I didn't.

Thisbe raises her arm for another potential karate chop

Oh yes I did! I know I did. How could I possibly forget! I'm certain of it! But if he'd not walked out in the first place, and if he'd only minded the machines as he was supposed to, and if he'd checked Revised Volume Six of the Cast List and not sent on the wrong Mourners, we wouldn't have lost him.
Pyramus Who?
Producer Orpheus.

Mrs Hawkins enters with a Plain-clothes Detective

We've lost him. He's gone into the Underworld.
Mrs Hawkins That's him! That's him! Arrest him!
Pyramus Who?
First Storyteller Him.
Producer Me?
Detective Just a few routine inquiries, sir. I'm from the Special Branch. Are you the Producer of this play?
Producer Me? Er—no! No! Good heavens, no! (*He points to Pyramus*) He is.
Mrs Hawkins I tell you it's him.
Detective Obstructing an Officer of the Law, that's one offence. (*He licks his pencil with relish and writes in his notebook*) I am making some inquiries into a kidnapping charge . . .
Producer I haven't kidnapped him, you silly clot!
Detective Insulting an Officer of the Law, that's two offences. (*He writes again*) Sticks and stones, remember, sticks and stones.
Mrs Hawkins Why don't you arrest him? He stole my boy!
Producer Borrowed.
Mrs Hawkins Stole.
Producer Borrowed.
Mrs Hawkins Stole.

The Detective writes in his book

Detective He borrowed a stole. And then what? Have you returned it?
Producer What?
Detective The stole you borrowed.
Producer What stole?
Mrs Hawkins My boy.
Producer Borrowed. (*He shakes his fist and gnashes his teeth*)

Detective Using threatening behaviour likely to cause a breach of the peace, that's three offences. I shall soon be Superintendent.

Thisbe We want to sue him for breach of contract.

Detective Four offences. I'm afraid you'll have to come along to the Police Station with me, sir, to answer certain charges made against you, and in particular the kidnapping of Orpheus Hawkins. He isn't here by any chance is he?

Harry Call Orpheus Hawkins.

Pyramus Orpheus Hawkins.

No answer

Detective No, I didn't think so, but in detective work, it's as well to check. Come along, then, sir.

Producer I resign! I resign!

They all leave except Mrs Hawkins

Mrs Hawkins That's all very well, but it still hasn't brought my boy back.

Faint music is heard

Orpheus enters from the back of the aisle C. *He walks in a trance-like state, with Eurydice some yards behind him*

Song: "O SPIRIT OF DEATH" (part reprise)

Orpheus (*singing*)
O spirit of life, give back once again
My love to the fields, the hills, and the rain.

O spirit of life, spirit of death,
Restore her to me, and to the green earth.

Mrs Hawkins stares down the aisle C *as if she can hardly believe her eyes*

She is with me. I must have faith. I must. I must not look back.

Mrs Hawkins Orpheus! Orpheus! Where have you been? Who is with you?

Orpheus does not appear to hear her, but climbs the steps of the apron. Eurydice emerges into the light

Orpheus! Has that Producer chap bewitched you? (*She comes forward and shakes Orpheus's arm*)

Orpheus awakens as if from a dream

Orpheus Oh, Mother! I am glad to see you. I'd like you to meet . . . (*He turns to Eurydice*)

Thunderclap. Complete Black-out

Oh, no. Eurydice. Oh, no! No! Eurydice! Eurydice! Come back. Come back!

A faint light. Orpheus lies prostrate and still on the stage, Eurydice and Mrs Hawkins have disappeared

Scene 6

The light brightens as the Third Storyteller enters, walks over to the proscenium arch and from the peg takes the coat belonging to the Second Storyteller

Third Storyteller And there it is. Sad, really. Strange are the workings of Fate. (*He puts on the coat*) It will be cold tonight: and I'll need this where I'm going. Good night.

The Third Storyteller crosses the stage in front of the prostrate figure of Orpheus and goes out. The Second Storyteller comes in. He stares at the empty peg

Second Storyteller Would you believe it! Somebody's pinched my coat. (*He turns and goes out the way he came in, calling*) Harry, have you seen my coat? (*In frustration at getting no answer*) Harry!

The Lights dim out at the end of the Play

the CURTAIN *falls*

FURNITURE AND PROPERTY LIST

ACT I

On stage: On *proscenium arch*: coat peg
Off stage: Tree-trunk seats and flowers (to be set during Black-out before
Scene 3)
Flower **(Thisbe)**
Fair stalls, Roller-Coaster entrance, paper hats, balloons, etc.
(Crowd)
Various suitable properties at discretion **(Jugglers, Magicians, etc.)**
Bass drum and stick. Large box **(Second Storyteller)**
Personal: **First Storyteller:** apple, script
Second Storyteller: coat, apple
Producer: whistle

ACT II

Set: Steps and levels at back of stage
Stone to represent throne
3 smaller thrones
Off stage: Skull
Lantern **(Third Storyteller)**
Banners **(Guards)**
3 wooden mallets **(Judges)**
Producer: military cap, officer's cane
Personal: **Detective:** notebook, pencil

LIGHTING PLOT

Property fittings required: nil
A bare stage

ACT I

To open: General lighting to cover stage

Cue 1   **Second Storyteller** exits   (Page 3)
        House lights up as gong sounds

Cue 2   **Producer** exits at end of Scene 2   (Page 6)
        Stage and house lights flicker and go out

Cue 3   As pastoral music starts   (Page 6)
        Bring up stage lights on woodland scene

Cue 4   At start of Scene 4   (Page 8)
        Bring stage lights up further

Cue 5   General exit at end of Scene 5   (Page 13)
        Flood stage with colourful light

Cue 6   At end of fairground scene   (Page 18)
        Lightning. Fade to Black-out, then up to dim, sinister light

Cue 7   **Eurydice** exits at end of Scene 7   (Page 19)
        Bring up stage lighting a little for dawn effect

Cue 8   **Orpheus** exits at end of Scene 8   (Page 19)
        Stage lights dim out. House lights up

ACT II

To open: Faint light on apron only. Brighten slowly through scene to represent harsh winter

Cue 9   **Orpheus** sits   (Page 20)
        Cross-fade spot on **Orpheus** *to spot on* **Third Storyteller**

Cue 10   **Third Storyteller:** ". . . or forget her"   (Page 21)
        Cross-fade to **Orpheus**

Cue 11   At end of Scene 1   (Page 22)
        Bring up general stage lighting

Cue 12   **Producer** and **Mrs Hawkins** exit   (Page 25)
        Dim stage lights. Bring up dim, shadowy effect as Scene 3 opens

Cue 13   **Orpheus** exits   (Page 26)
        Bring up "black light" for ballet

Cue 14   **Orpheus:** "Monstrous, monstrous."   (Page 26)
        Bring up red glow

Cue 15   **Orpheus** and **Third Storyteller** exit   (Page 27)
            Cross-fade to Hades' Kingdom lighting—dim and weird

Cue 16   **Hades** and **Procession** exit   (Page 30)
            Dim stage lights—bring up for Scene 5 when ready

Cue 17   **Orpheus** turns to Eurydice   (Page 33)
            Black-out

Cue 18   **Orpheus:** "Come back. Come back!"   (Page 33)
            Bring up dim lighting

Cue 19   **Orpheus** lies prostrate. **Third Storyteller** enters   (Page 34)
            Dim light on **Orpheus,** *cross-fade to bright spot on* **Third
            Storyteller**

Cue 20   **Second Storyteller:** ". . . have you seen my coat?"   (Page 34)
            Fade to Black-out

EFFECTS PLOT

ACT I

Cue 1   As Scene 1 ends   (Page 3)
            Rocket explosion, voices singing 'Nymphs and Shepherds',
               then sounds of express train and dinner gong

Cue 2   **Producer** exits   (Page 4)
            Brass band music, fade on **Producer**'s *re-entry*

Cue 3   As Scene 2 ends   (Page 6)
            Marching feet, gong, loudspeaker announcement, followed
               by a crash, groans—the silence

Cue 4   Following Cue 3   (Page 6)
            Music—a gay pastoral

Cue 5   Voice: "... Orpheus, Orpheus."   (Page 7)
            Hollow, mocking laugh

Cue 6   **Producer:** "Merry-go-round ready?"   (Page 11)
            Few bars of "Carousel Waltz" on loudspeaker

Cue 7   **Producer:** "Steamboat ready?"   (Page 11)
            Hiss of steam, then boiling kettle

Cue 8   **Producer:** "Barrel-organ ready?"   (Page 11)
            Popping and gurgling noise, then drunken voice

Cue 9   At start of Scene 6   (Page 13)
            Gong, then fairground music

Cue 10   **Thisbe:** "Oh, maim 'im, etc."   (Page 17)
            Sound of Roller-Coaster

Cue 11   At end of fairground scene   (Page 18)
            Thunder and wind—fade as **Eurydice** *lies still*

Cue 12   Four **Underworld Mourners** enter   (Page 18)
            Loud whispering sound through speaker

Cue 13   At start of Scene 8   (Page 19)
            Bird song

Cue 14   **Orpheus** exits   (Page 19)
            Fade bird song

ACT II

Cue 15   **Producer** and **Mrs Hawkins** exit   Page 25)
            Loud crash, low moan, followed by foreboding music

Cue 16   **Charon** enters   (Page 25)
            Sound of lapping water—continue until **Charon** *exits*

Cue 17   **Orpheus:** "Monstrous, monstrous."   (Page 26)
            Groans, shrieks

NOTES ON PRONUNCIATION

AEACUS ē′a-kus;   ARISTAEUS ăr″ĭs-tē′us;   CALLIOPE ka-lī′ō-pē;
CHARON kā′rŏn;   EURYDICE ū-rĭd′ĭ-sē;   HADES hā′dēz;
MINOS mī′nŏs;   ORPHEUS ôr′fūs or ôr′fē-us;   PYRAMUS pĭr′a-mŭs;
RHADAMANTHUS r″ăda-măn′thus;   THISBE thĭz′bē

ā as in *fate*; ă as in *fat*; *a* as in *comma*; ē as in *see*; ī as in *bite*; ĭ as in *hit*; ō as
in *dole*; ŏ as in *not*; ô as in *orb*; ū as in *cue*; ŭ as in *but*; *u* as in *circus*; *th* as in
thing; ′ = primary accent; ″ = secondary accent

MADE AND PRINTED IN GREAT BRITAIN BY
LATIMER TREND & COMPANY LTD PLYMOUTH